KENYA

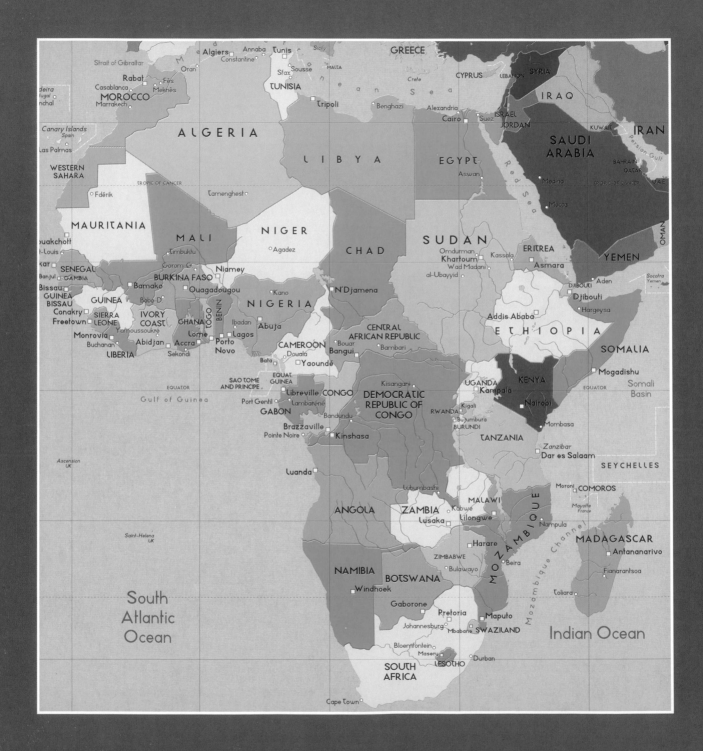

KENYA

Jim Corrigan

Mason Crest Publishers
Philadelphia

Produced by OTTN Publishing, Stockton, N.J.

Mason Crest Publishers
370 Reed Road
Broomall, PA 19008
www.masoncrest.com

3 5 7 9 8 6 4 2

Library of Congress Cataloging-in-Publication Data

Corrigan, Jim.
  Kenya / Jim Corrigan.
      p. cm. — (Africa)
  Includes bibliographical references and index.
  ISBN 1-59084-809-8
  1. Kenya—Juvenile literature. I. Title. II. Series.

  DT433.522.C67 2004
  967.62—dc22

                                                          2004007105

Africa:
Facts and Figures

Burundi

**Democratic Republic
of the Congo**

Ethiopia

Ghana

Ivory Coast

Kenya

Nigeria

Rwanda

South Africa

Tanzania

Uganda

Zimbabwe

Table of Contents

Introduction   6
Robert I. Rotberg

Cradle of Humankind   11

From Nomads to Nationalists   19

Stability, Corruption, and Democracy   29

Striving for Economic Recovery   37

One Nation, Many Cultures   47

A Tour of the Cities   59

A Calendar of Kenyan Festivals   66

Recipes   68

Glossary   70

Project and Report Ideas   72

Chronology   74

Further Reading/Internet Resources   76

For More Information   77

Index   78

Africa: Continent in the Balance
Robert I. Rotberg

Africa is the cradle of humankind, but for millennia it was off the familiar, beaten path of global commerce and discovery. Its many peoples therefore developed largely apart from the diffusion of modern knowledge and the spread of technological innovation until the 17th through 19th centuries. With the coming to Africa of the book, the wheel, the hoe, and the modern rifle and cannon, foreigners also brought the vastly destructive transatlantic slave trade, oppression, discrimination, and onerous colonial rule. Emerging from that crucible of European rule, Africans created nationalistic movements and then claimed their numerous national independences in the 1960s. The result is the world's largest continental assembly of new countries.

There are 53 members of the African Union, a regional political grouping, and 48 of those nations lie south of the Sahara. Fifteen of them, including mighty Ethiopia, are landlocked, making international trade and economic growth that much more arduous and expensive. Access to navigable rivers is limited, natural harbors are few, soils are poor and thin, several countries largely consist of miles and miles of sand, and tropical diseases have sapped the strength and productivity of innumerable millions. Being landlocked, having few resources (although countries along Africa's west coast have tapped into deep offshore petroleum and gas reservoirs), and being beset by malaria, tuberculosis, schistosomiasis, AIDS, and many other maladies has kept much of Africa poor for centuries.

Thirty-two of the world's poorest 44 countries are African. Hunger is common. So is rapid deforestation and desertification. Unemployment rates are often over 50 percent, for jobs are few—even in agriculture. Where Africa once

Kenya, which borders the Indian Ocean in East Africa, attracts tourists with its vast array of plants and wildlife.

was a land of small villages and a few large cities, with almost everyone engaged in growing grain or root crops or grazing cattle, camels, sheep, and goats, today more than half of all the more than 750 million Africans, especially those who live south of the Sahara, reside in towns and cities. Traditional agriculture hardly pays, and a number of countries in Africa—particularly the smaller and more fragile ones—can no longer feed themselves.

There is not one Africa, for the continent is full of contradictions and variety. Of the 675 million people living south of the Sahara, at least 130 million live in Nigeria, 67 million in Ethiopia, 55 million in the Democratic Republic of

A lone tree stands in the Masai Mara Game Reserve in Kenya.

the Congo, and 45 million in South Africa. By contrast, tiny Djibouti and Equatorial Guinea have fewer than 1 million people each, and prosperous Botswana and Namibia each are under 2 million in population. Within some countries, even medium-sized ones like Zambia (11 million), there are a plethora of distinct ethnic groups speaking separate languages. Zambia, typical with its multitude of competing entities, has 70 such peoples, roughly broken down into four language and cultural zones. Three of those languages jostle with English for primacy.

Given the kaleidoscopic quality of African culture and deep-grained poverty, it is no wonder that Africa has developed economically and politically less rapidly than other regions. Since independence from colonial rule, weak governance has also plagued Africa and contributed significantly to the widespread poverty of its peoples. Only Botswana and offshore Mauritius have been governed democratically without interruption since independence. Both are among Africa's wealthiest countries, too, thanks to the steady application of good governance.

Aside from those two nations, and South Africa, Africa has been a continent of coups since 1960, with massive and oil-rich Nigeria suffering incessant periods of harsh, corrupt, autocratic military rule. Nearly every other country on or around the continent, small and large, has been plagued by similar bouts of instability and dictatorial rule. In the 1970s and 1980s Idi Amin ruled Uganda capriciously and Jean-Bedel Bokassa proclaimed himself emperor of the Central African Republic. Macias Nguema of Equatorial Guinea was another in that same mold. More recently Daniel arap Moi held Kenya in thrall and Robert Mugabe has imposed himself on once-prosperous Zimbabwe. In both of those cases, as in the case of Gnassingbe Eyadema in Togo and the late Mobutu Sese Seko in Congo, these presidents stole wildly and drove entire peoples and their nations into penury. Corruption is common in Africa, and so are a weak rule-of-law framework, misplaced development, high expenditures on soldiers and low expenditures on health and education, and a widespread (but not universal) refusal on the part of leaders to work well for their followers and citizens.

Conflict between groups within countries has also been common in Africa. More than 12 million Africans have been killed in the civil wars of Africa since 1990, with more than 3 million losing their lives in Congo and more than 2 million in the Sudan. War between north and south has been constant in the Sudan since 1981. In 2003 there were serious ongoing hostilities in northeastern Congo, Burundi, Angola, Liberia, Guinea, Ivory Coast, the Central African Republic, and Guinea-Bissau, and a coup (later reversed) in São Tomé and Príncipe.

Despite such dangers, despotism, and decay, Africa is improving. Botswana and Mauritius, now joined by South Africa, Senegal, Kenya, and Ghana, are beacons of democratic growth and enlightened rule. Uganda and Senegal are taking the lead in combating and reducing the spread of AIDS, and others are following. There are serious signs of the kinds of progressive economic policy changes that might lead to prosperity for more of Africa's peoples. The trajectory in Africa is positive.

Many anthropologists believe humans originated in Kenya. Fossil evidence indicates that prehistoric man traveled, hunted, and developed customs in groups. (Opposite) A group of young Nandi warriors in the Rift Valley. (Right) Mount Kenya, an extinct volcano, has snow and ice year-round.

1 Cradle of Humankind

MILLIONS OF YEARS AGO, humanity's earliest ancestors roamed the diverse landscape of Kenya. In fact, many anthropologists and archaeologists believe Kenya is where the human species first originated.

Kenya is extraordinary in many other ways. The country contains virtually every type of terrain imaginable, from tropical shores to snow-capped mountains. Kenya's diverse landscape hosts a remarkable variety of plant and animal life. The Kenyan people are also diverse. Over 40 languages are spoken within the country's borders, and lifestyles range from cosmopolitan to rustic. Older Kenyans have known both the oppression of colonial rule and the thrill of national independence. Though the country is not without serious problems, including widespread government corruption, it is regarded as a model of stability for many of its troubled African neighbors.

Geographical Features

Kenya is a Texas-sized swath of land in East Africa. It straddles the equator and is bordered by Ethiopia and Sudan in the north, Uganda in the west, Tanzania in the south, and Somalia and the Indian Ocean in the east. Stretching from Kenya's sandy beaches and tropical jungles along the Indian Ocean, the landscape gradually rises. Hot, arid plains slowly give way to grassy slopes and tree-covered mountains.

The country's southwestern corner contains a portion of Lake Victoria, which next to Lake Superior is the largest freshwater lake in the world. The shallow and narrow Lake Turkana (formerly Lake Rudolf) lies in the country's north. Between these impressive bodies of water runs a topographical depression known as the Great Rift Valley, which is believed to have been formed tens of millions of years ago when an unstable section of the earth's crust collapsed amid violent tremors.

The same geological activity responsible for the Great Rift Valley also created numerous volcanoes in Kenya, nearly all of which are now extinct. The remnants of one such volcano, Mount Kenya, stands at 17,057 feet (5,199 meters). It is so tall that today its upper slopes are always covered with snow and ice.

While they were active, these volcanoes and corresponding earthquakes gradually transformed western Kenya from a flat, forested plain into a series of fertile highlands. Rainwater flowed down from the newly formed mountains, creating rivers and lakes. Regions denied rainfall by the larger mountains became hot, dry grasslands called *savannas*. Other areas turned into desert. To the east, Kenya's 333 miles (536 kilometers) of coastline along the Indian Ocean remained tropical.

Kenya has two rainy seasons: the "long rains," which last from March until June, and the "short rains," which last from October to December. Whenever there is not enough precipitation during the rainy seasons, a drought usually occurs. The amount of rainfall varies by ecological zone. For example, the tropical coast receives an average of 41 inches (104 centimeters) per year, while the desert regions average just 13 inches (33 cm) each year. Likewise, the temperature range varies between regions. Steamy coastal

Quick Facts: The Geography of Kenya

Location: Eastern Africa, bordering the Indian Ocean, between Somalia and Tanzania
Area: (slightly more than twice the size of Nevada)
  total: 224,903 square miles (582,650 sq km)
  land: 219,731 square miles (569,250 sq km)
  water: 5,172 square miles (13,400 sq km)
Borders: Ethiopia, 535 miles (861 km); Somalia, 424 miles (682 km); Sudan, 144 miles (232 km), Tanzania, 478 miles (769 km); Uganda, 580 miles (933 km); coastline, 333 miles (536 km)

Climate: varies from tropical along coast to arid in interior
Terrain: low plains rise to central highlands bisected by Great Rift Valley; fertile plateau in west
Elevation extremes:
  lowest point: Indian Ocean, 0 feet
  highest point: Mount Kenya, 17,057 feet (5,199 meters)
Natural hazards: recurring drought; flooding during rainy seasons

Source: CIA World Factbook, 2003.

areas rarely experience temperatures below 68°F (20°C) while the mile-high capital city of Nairobi, located in the highlands, can cool down to 45°F (7°C) at night. Peak temperatures across the country range from 79°F (26°C) to 99°F (37°C), depending on location and time of year. Kenya's warmest month is January and its coolest month is July.

Plants and Animals

People come from around the world to see the country's extraordinary wildlife, including some species that are *indigenous* only to Kenya. For some of these species, Kenya's national parks and sanctuaries serve as a final chance to avoid extinction. The African black rhinoceros, for instance, was virtually hunted into oblivion for its prized horns in the 1970s and 1980s. By 1989, there were only 330 black rhinos left in Kenya. Now closely monitored and protected by park rangers, the black rhino population has returned to about 500, or a quarter of the world's population. While this is encouraging, the species is still in grave danger of disappearing forever.

Heavily hunted for its ivory tusks, the African elephant also experienced a marked population decline in the 1970s and 1980s. Fortunately, the elephant has rebounded faster than the rhino, and today's elephant population in Kenya exceeds 27,000. It can be found throughout the country, wherever there is an ample supply of food and water.

Kenya's wide variety of herbivores includes over 30 species of antelope, vast herds of which can be seen grazing the highlands. Each year in August and September, over a million *wildebeest* migrate into southern Kenya from Tanzania. Seeking fresh grass brought on by the rainy seasons, the wildebeest cross crocodile-infested rivers and brave other dangers. Observing their journey is a popular pastime for tourists.

Surprisingly, the plant-eating hippopotamus is responsible for more human deaths in Kenya each year than any other animal. The hippo spends its days drifting through rivers and lakes. Although it has a docile appearance, it will tip any boat that draws too near, then lunge at the occupants inside.

More than 1,100 types of birds have been recorded in Kenya (compared to about 850 in all of North America). This figure includes native species as

A rhinoceros grazes at Sweetwaters Game Reserve in Kenya. The black rhino in particular is in danger of becoming extinct, and reserves like this one help bring the population numbers back up.

well as the millions of birds that migrate to Kenya annually from as far away as Scandinavia. The country's wide variety of habitats provides an ideal winter home for nearly every type of bird.

The deadliest reptiles in Kenya are the Nile crocodiles, which prowl the lakes and rivers in search of food. The country's many venomous snakes can be just as lethal. Over 100 varieties of lizard also reside in Kenya, ranging

Kenya's wildlife and natural parks are attractive to tourists, and approximately a million people visited the country in 2002. However, the threat of terrorism has caused the number of tourists who visit Kenya to decline over the past few years.

from the tiny pygmy chameleon to the 6-foot (2-meter) Nile monitor. The former eats small insects while the latter spends its time scavenging along riverbanks for crocodile eggs.

Nobody knows exactly how many different types of plants grow in Kenya, but the figure is believed to be somewhere around 10,000. Only scrub appears in the low-lying desert areas that receive very little rain, and at slightly higher altitudes, arid grasslands are broken up by the occasional shrub or tree. However, in the Kenyan highlands, forest and robust grasslands prevail with the greatest variety of flora. Above 12,000 feet (3,650 meters) is an alpine environment with giant trees and hearty shrubs and grasses.

Unspoiled land has always been Kenya's greatest natural resource. Sadly, this national asset is rapidly deteriorating under the weight of human expansion. Widespread deforestation for farming purposes has led to soil erosion; excessive use of fertilizers and pesticides has polluted water supplies; and some species of wildlife, such as the elephant and rhino, have fallen victim to *poaching*. Virtually all species have seen their habitats altered in some way by human intervention. Most recently, the introduction of the water hyacinth, a tropical weed, to Lake Victoria has threatened native plants and fish.

Despite the steps taken by the Kenyan government in recent decades, these and other environmental threats persist. A longstanding tradition of public corruption has frequently led the government to turn a blind eye on harmful, illicit activities performed for profit.

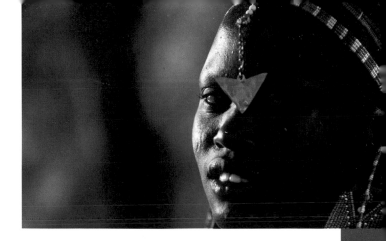

(Opposite) Two young women stand outside their hut, West Pokot. (Right) A Masai woman wears a traditional headdress. The Masai are known for their beadwork, and the colors and patterns of this headdress indicate the wearer's age and status in the tribe.

2 From Nomads to Nationalists

THE REPUBLIC OF KENYA has existed for less than half a century. For 80 years prior, it was a British colony. There is little that is known about the country before colonization. Ancient fossils, some as old as 8 million years, and local legend passed down through generations only provide a sketch of Kenya's early history.

Prehistoric humans are known to have hunted in the East African savannas with stone weapons as far back as 2.5 million years ago or perhaps earlier. According to scientists, around 10,000 years ago hunter-gatherers began living together and migrating with the seasons. Cultures began encountering one another and often merged, combining languages and customs. Roughly 2,000 years ago, a collection of languages known as Bantu became prevalent in the south and west. Arab traders later arrived on the coast and their language mixed with Bantu to form a new tongue called Swahili.

Because they had closer contact with the outside world, the Swahili soon possessed many more materials than the inland peoples had. Ships from the Middle East, India, and China sailed into ports bringing cloth, ceramics, and sugar, which were traded for ivory, animal skins, and slaves. For several centuries, Arab and Swahili communities thrived all along the Kenyan coastline.

Arrival of the Europeans

In 1498, Portuguese explorer Vasco da Gama landed at the coastal city of Malindi while mapping a sea route to India. The Portuguese were welcomed there, but the reception they received from rulers at other ports was far less than hospitable. The Portuguese government responded by sending raiding parties virtually everywhere except Malindi. By the close of the 16th century, Portugal had established a solid presence along the coast.

Portuguese rule in that particular region was harsh. As a result, throughout much of the 17th century regular uprisings occurred that slowly drained the conquerors' will to dominate the region. In 1696, a 33-month siege of Fort Jesus in the town of Mombasa left hundreds dead and persuaded Portugal to begin withdrawing from the region. After the conflict, the Swahili enjoyed a period of freedom from foreign oppression. But by the 1840s, European missionaries began arriving in the area, and soldiers followed behind them. Soon, in western Kenya and neighboring Uganda tribesmen were captured for the slave trade and exported to Arabia and the Indian Ocean Islands.

Britain and Germany sought to establish colonies in East Africa, and so in

1885 they agreed to split territorial control of the region. Under the agreement, Germany received possession of present-day Tanzania and Britain took control of Uganda and Kenya. At the time, Uganda seemed like the greater prize to the British, while Kenya had a bad reputation for its wild animals and hostile tribes, particularly the aggressive Masai people. However, the explorers and missionaries already settled in Kenya began making reports of its economic potential to compatriots back home. After the British East Africa Company was founded in 1887, with its headquarters established in Mombasa, the company launched projects to advance trade in the region. Construction soon began on the railway from Mombasa to Lake Victoria.

The Portuguese explorer Vasco da Gama was the first European to reach East Africa by sea. His 1497–99 voyage showed the way to the Indian Ocean, and within 25 years Portugal controlled important ports on the East African and Indian coasts.

The 581-mile (935-kilometer) railway took six years to build at a tremendous financial—and human—cost. Britain had imported 32,000 laborers from India, another of its colonies, to build the railway. Hundreds died during its construction, falling victim to accidents, lion attacks, or poison arrows. Meanwhile, the British established a supply depot on the banks of the Nairobi River, and this staging area gradually developed into Nairobi. The railway's completion achieved the intended effect of strengthening British control.

The new rail line had a second and perhaps more profound impact: it made Kenya's fertile highlands more easily accessible. British settlers began to arrive and the colonial government was more than happy to give them tracts of land. The natives were pushed off the best ground to make way for white farmers. The colonists passed laws that permitted only the settlers to grow cash crops such as coffee and tea, while natives were forced to either grow less profitable crops or work on the white-owned farms. The highland-dwelling *Kikuyu* peoples suffered the most from this incursion.

When World War I broke out in 1914, tens of thousands of Kenyan males were drafted into the British army and fought with the settlers against the Germans in Tanzania. When the war was over, the white soldiers were rewarded with land and as a result, the settler population grew to 9,000. The Kenyan soldiers, on the other hand, only lost more of their land and continued to face strict colonial laws. British taxes on Kenyans' meager huts further angered the local population. The seeds of rebellion had been sown.

Rebellion and Independence

By the end of World War I, British settlers had gained a great deal of influence in East Africa. The territory was officially named Kenya in 1920, and a colonial government was established. Colonial administrators maintained power by keeping ethnic groups separated and suspicious of one another. Kenyans continued to pay high taxes, which forced many of them to work on the Europeans' plantations for very low wages. Blacks were not allowed to vote or serve in the colonial legislature.

Educated Kenyans were upset about the government's unfair policies and began to protest. Political organizations formed to rally for such causes as the return of lands taken by European settlers and Kenyan representation in the colonial government. One of the early leaders in this movement was a mission-educated Nairobi resident named Jomo Kenyatta.

During the 1920s and 1930s, most Kenyans wished to remain part of the British Empire and focused their protests on ending discrimination and unfair laws. After World War II, however, *nationalist* movements swept through British colonies in Africa and other parts of the empire. In Kenya the Swahili word *uhuru*, which means "freedom," became popular as people talked for the first time of an independent Kenyan nation. Kenyatta became an ardent nationalist and with his supporters attempted to unify the many different Kenyan organizations seeking independence. Out of this campaign for unity, the Kenyan African Union (KAU) was founded in 1944.

A new wave of European settlement in Kenya finally sparked a violent revolt. Just as in the past, these settlers had been apportioned Kenya's most fertile land. In response, young Kikuyu men who had been displaced from their homelands resurrected an oath-taking tradition and secretly swore themselves as enemies of the British. Many were veterans who had learned guerilla warfare while fighting for the British army during World War II. The movement came to be known as the Mau Mau Rebellion.

The Mau Mau Rebellion raged for most of the 1950s. In 1952, the colonial government declared a state of emergency and arrested 83 Kenyan leaders, including Kenyatta, on charges of encouraging revolt. Mau Mau fighters retreated to the jungle and staged surprise attacks at night. British troops poured into Kenya to quell the uprising, and the government recruited

Members of the Kikuyu tribe suspected of participating in the Mau Mau Rebellion are held in the Thompson Falls prison camp. More than 10,000 Kenyans, mostly Kikuyu, died in prison camps as the British tried to put down the rebellion.

Kenyans to fight the Mau Mau, turning the rebellion into a genuine civil war. The Mau Mau were eventually defeated, and the state of emergency was lifted in 1960. Over 13,000 Kenyans—primarily Kikuyu—had died, while fewer than 100 British soldiers and settlers were killed.

Though a military failure, the Mau Mau rebellion persuaded Britain that colonial rule was no longer feasible in Kenya. The British made preparations to grant the colony its independence; Jomo Kenyatta was released from prison; and a provisional Kenyan government was formed in 1961. Many white settlers, fearing retribution, sold their farms and returned to Europe. On December 12, 1963, the new flag of Kenya was raised in Nairobi. One year later, Kenya officially became a republic, with Kenyatta as its president.

The Modern Era

Land reform was a top priority for the young Kenyan government. The sprawling highland farms of white settlers were purchased and then divided into smaller parcels for thousands of peasants. Economic growth soon followed, and the country's standard of living gradually improved. However, it quickly became apparent that Kenya's numerous ethnic groups were jockeying for power and control. The Kikuyu, in particular, had a fast-growing presence in government, business, and the military. The first decade of the Uhuru (Freedom) Movement in Kenya was blemished by political schisms, economic disparity, and several assassinations.

The government fell into corruption, with President Kenyatta rumored to have amassed extraordinary personal wealth. Impoverished Kenyans recognized that life had barely improved since independence, and civil disorder returned. Kenyatta withdrew into seclusion, and in 1978 he grew ill and died. Vice President Daniel arap Moi assumed temporary control and was elected president several months later.

Moi spoke fondly about the early years of Kenyatta's leadership and promised a return to government accountability. During the first few months of his administration, Moi kept that promise by cracking down on corruption, discouraging ethnic favoritism, and releasing political prisoners.

Nationalist leader Jomo Kenyatta spent time in jail during the Mau Mau rebellion. When Britain relinquished control over Kenya, Kenyatta became the first president of the newly independent republic.

However, he also refused to make the necessary economic changes.

In August 1982, a small contingent of the Kenyan Air Force launched a coup against President Moi. By day's end, the government had easily put down the coup and 12 airmen were sentenced to death. Moi used the attempted takeover as an excuse to crack down on his political opponents and threw a number of them in prison. He spent the remainder of the 1980s and much of the 1990s consolidating power, forcibly silencing his critics and accumulating personal wealth.

By this time, Kenya had grown dependent on foreign aid to keep its economy running. Donor nations such as the United States and Britain became concerned with Moi's dictatorial tendencies, and on several occasions the International Monetary Fund withheld aid payments. To have the foreign aid reinstated, Moi instituted reforms and held multiparty elections in 1992. But the changes fell short of genuine reform, and the results of the elections, which were marred by ethnic violence, were dubious at best.

Forces from outside the country were also threatening its stability. Several terrorist groups became active in the 1990s and began staging attacks around the globe. The most notable of these groups was al-Qaeda, a worldwide terrorist network led by Saudi-born Osama bin Laden. In August 1998, al-Qaeda car-bombed the U.S. Embassy in Nairobi, killing 219 people and wounding several thousand. Most of the casualties were Kenyan workers. Terrorists struck again in November 2002, when al-Qaeda operatives drove a vehicle packed with explosives into a coastal resort hotel in Mombasa, killing ten Kenyans and three Israeli tourists.

Amid this turmoil, Kenyans went to the voting polls in December 2002 to elect a new president. The people overwhelmingly chose Mwai Kibaki, a former economics professor who ran on a *rainbow coalition* platform of integrity and accountability. Both Kenyan and international observers called Kibaki's election an important first step in advancing the nation toward democracy.

As Kenya's government became corrupt, leading to violent demonstrations and protests, Kenyatta went into seclusion. After his death in 1978, Daniel arap Moi (in photograph) became president. Although he initially promised a return to government accountability, Moi never took any steps toward genuine reform.

(Opposite) Government buildings are located on Government Road in Nairobi. (Right) Outgoing president Daniel arap Moi sits to the right of the president-elect, Mwai Kibaki, during his swearing-in ceremony, December 30, 2002. As president, Kibaki promised to crack down on the corruption and poverty that had plagued previous administrations.

3 Stability, Corruption, and Democracy

LIKE MOST COUNTRIES committed to preserving democracy, Kenya has three separate government branches that monitor each other's practices. While the president plays a pivotal role in shaping the government, the legislature is also responsible to establish laws and policies, and the judiciary to enforce those laws and policies.

To win a presidential election, a candidate must receive the largest number of overall votes and 25 percent or more of the vote in at least five of the country's eight administrative regions (seven provinces and one area set aside for Nairobi). Otherwise, a runoff election is held. Once elected, the president enjoys broad powers: he or she chooses the vice president, appoints the chief justice, and nominates 12 members of the legislature.

The 224-seat legislature is referred to either as the National Assembly or the Bunge. As with the presidency, elections to the Bunge are held every five years. At the local level, a commissioner heads each of Kenya's 69 districts, which fall within the seven provinces.

The Kenyan legal system is a blend of British, Islamic, and tribal law. British law stresses the rights of the accused; Islamic law is based on the teachings of the prophet Muhammad; and tribal law is shaped by the indigenous practices and customs that have developed over the centuries. Cases are decided by judges and magistrates, not juries. Kenya's judicial system has long been home to corruption and will surely remain under close scrutiny for some time to come. In late 2003, a government probe led to the suspension of 23 judges for unethical conduct. There was also evidence of corruption found against another 130 judges, who were placed under investigation.

A small volunteer military provides for the country's defense. The combined strength of the army, navy, and air force is less than 25,000 personnel. Because these armed forces are small, keeping close relationships with other nations is an important part of Kenya's defense strategy. Like most East African nations seeking to combat terrorism, Kenya has received military training and support from the United States in recent years.

With the possible exceptions of education and health care, the Kenyan government provides little in the way of social services. Instead, Kenyans rely on their families and a longstanding tradition known as **harambee**, which literally means "pulling together." Through *harambee*, communities raise money for public construction and other functions normally handled by the government. Wealthy and influential residents make large contributions at fund-raising events, hoping to inspire others to do the same.

Harambee was championed by Jomo Kenyatta, and is likely to remain an integral part of community development. But it also has its critics, who point out that donations made by the rich are often self-serving, intended only to buy publicity and prestige. The critics argue further that precious financial resources could be spent more efficiently if they were overseen at a national level, rather than through hundreds of individual, uncoordinated projects. In 2003, the government banned public officials from managing *harambees*, following the outbreak of several scandals in which donated money was not used for its intended purpose. However, in February 2004 many legislators declared they would continue to manage *harambees* despite the new law.

Politics and Corruption

Kenya's first organized political parties appeared in the 1920s. The most influential of these was the Kikuyu Central Association (KCA), which lobbied for the return of land lost to settlers. The KCA was banned in the 1930s and a decade later was succeeded by the Kenyan African Union (KAU), led by Jomo Kenyatta. This group was outlawed in the 1950s during the Mau Mau Rebellion. After the country's independence in 1963, the Kenya African National Union (KANU) emerged as the dominant political party. KANU grew so powerful under the leadership of President Daniel arap Moi that in 1982 Kenya officially became a one-party state.

The mounting internal and external demands for democracy forced the government to introduce a multiparty system in 1991. However, the new organizations were divided and proved no match for KANU's well-oiled political machine. The opposition candidates, who included Mwai Kibaki of the

Supporters of the National Rainbow Coalition (NARC) celebrate the election of Kibaki as president in December 2002. This marked the first time in Kenya's history that the candidate of the Kenyan African National Union (KANU) was out of power.

Democratic Party, were soundly defeated and Moi remained in power. He was reelected to another five-year term in 1997 amid significant fraud and violence.

The 2002 presidential election offered a tremendous opportunity for change. Moi would be forced to step down, having served the maximum number of terms permitted by law. By this time, the opposition parties had banded together to form the National Rainbow Coalition (NARC) with Kibaki as its candidate. He won handily, capturing 63 percent of the vote. On December 30, 2002, more than 200,000 people turned out in Nairobi to see their first new leader in more than two decades sworn into office.

Even critics of Kenya's government admit that it compares favorably with other African nations. Power struggles have been few and relatively free of violence. Government-provided services, while sparse, have at least been reliable. And Kenya has been unaffected, for the most part, by the chaos in neighboring countries such as Somalia and Sudan.

However, a legacy of fraud and bribery has cursed Kenya's public administration virtually since the time of independence. Elected officials and civil servants have always demanded *kitu-kidogo*, Swahili for "a little something," and many Kenyans long ago resigned themselves to paying the bribes. Among the worst offenders are police officers, who have been known to set up roadblocks in order to collect payments from taxis.

At the start of 2003, the German-based watchdog group Transparency International released a study tracking bribery and corruption within Kenya. The survey found that two out of three encounters with Kenyan public officials resulted in a bribe request, and that citizens paid an average of $16 per month (a sizable sum for most Kenyans) in bribes to police officers alone.

President Kibaki's first step in fighting *graft* was the creation of an ethics office to monitor the government's dealings. Next he introduced a bill requiring politicians to publicly disclose their finances. A special commission would investigate and prosecute those who have abused their public office. Within Kibaki's first month in office, a judge accused of taking a $6,700 bribe two years earlier was arrested. Kenyans responded enthusiastically to the anti-corruption campaign, refusing to pay the customary *kitu-kidogo* and reporting those officials who requested it.

Whether this fundamental change in Kenyan government is permanent or only temporary remains to be seen. So far, the results seem positive. In the *Kenya Bribery Index 2004*, Transparency International reported a significant decrease in bribery. The number of cases in which bribes were demanded dropped to four in ten. However, the average size of bribes increased by about

50 percent. "This trend . . . lends itself to two interpretations," indicated the report. "First, it suggests a significant reduction in petty bribery. Second, it is also consistent with the perception of increased likelihood of being punished if caught, hence officials require bigger inducement to take the risk."

Wildlife Conservation

In 1989, the government began taking an active role in preserving Kenya's most valuable national resource with the creation of the Kenya Wildlife Service (KWS). Paleontologist and conservationist Richard Leakey was the organization's first leader. Leakey came from a famous family of archaeologists in Kenya. In the 1920s his parents, Louis and Mary, unearthed the first prehistoric fossils that suggested Kenya was the birthplace of humanity. Richard continued the work of his parents, which culminated with his 1984 discovery of an ancient skeleton near Lake Turkana. The skeleton was that of the species *Homo erectus*, a direct predecessor to modern man.

Richard Leakey was dedicated as KWS director, vowing to halt the epidemic of elephant and rhino poaching that was plaguing Kenya. He sent armed teams into the national parks with orders to find and arrest poachers, or shoot those who resisted. He organized press conferences at which large stockpiles of confiscated ivory were burned. He turned away bribes and ensured that no KWS employee would accept one, either. Soon the poachers disappeared and the elephant and rhino populations began to recover.

Leakey's honest and aggressive style of management stood in sharp contrast to typical government practices during the 1990s. As a result, he earned many enemies. Several high-ranking officials made allegations of mismanagement and corruption at KWS. The charges were baseless, but recognizing that his adversaries would stop at nothing, Leakey announced his resignation from KWS and entered politics. The new KWS director lacked the aggressive leadership skills of his predecessor. Poachers began to reappear and park revenues plummeted. When foreign donations began to dry up in 1998, the government had no choice but to reinstall Leakey as the KWS director.

Currently, KWS is modifying its underlying philosophy. While Leakey, who has since resigned as director, always believed that Kenya's national parks should be closed ecosystems, KWS and other organizations now believe that humans and wildlife can coexist and even thrive together under the proper regulations. Accordingly, new policies focus more on modifying human behavior within the parks rather than keeping people out. This approach, while progressive, has led to more frequent incidents with wildlife, particularly the big cats.

Kenya remains committed to ensuring the health of its ecology for several reasons, one of which is its impact on tourism, a pivotal industry of the Kenyan economy. Overseeing dozens of wildlife parks and reserves, KWS has a caretaker role that is crucial to the economy and Kenya's overall stability.

Famed paleontologist Richard Leakey, shown here in his early career holding the skull of a hominid found at Lake Rudolph, was the first leader of the Kenya Wildlife Service (KWS). His influence kept endangered animals living in national parks safe from poachers.

Agriculture has always been an important source of income for Kenyans. (Opposite) Women harvest tea on their family farm to sell. (Right) A greenhouse worker in the Lake Naivasha region holds roses. Kenya has become the leading supplier of cut flowers to Europe, sending more than 300 million stems a year of different types of flowers.

4 Striving for Economic Recovery

PRIOR TO INDEPENDENCE, the Kenyan economy was geared toward producing agricultural exports. White settlers grew profitable crops such as coffee and tea, and the native population was encouraged to work on the settler farms. Eventually, black farmers were permitted to grow cash crops on a limited basis, and following independence, their role increased dramatically. Significant foreign involvement in Kenyan agriculture remained a constant, however, and still does today.

The 1960s and 1970s were marked by healthy economic growth for the fledgling nation. The government welcomed foreign investment and endeavored to educate its largely unskilled workforce. Fueled by stunning gains in agricultural production, Kenya's economy grew at a cumulative rate of 6.8 percent between 1963 and 1980, among the highest in Africa. Foreign investment and technology flowed into the country even faster

Quick Facts: The Economy of Kenya

Gross domestic product (GDP*):
$32.89 billion

Inflation: 1.9%

Natural resources: gold, limestone, soda ash, salt, rubies, fluorspar, garnets, wildlife, hydropower

Agriculture (24% of GDP): tea, coffee, corn, wheat, sugarcane, fruit, vegetables, dairy products, beef, pork, poultry, eggs (2001 est.)

Industry (13% of GDP): small-scale consumer goods (plastic, furniture, batteries, textiles, soap, cigarettes, flour), agricultural products processing, oil refining, cement, tourism (2001 est.)

Services (63% of GDP): government, other (2001 est.)

Foreign Trade:
Exports—$2.1 billion: tea, horticultural products, coffee, petroleum products, fish, cement
Imports—$3 billion: machinery and transportation equipment, petroleum products, motor vehicles, iron and steel, resins and plastics

Economic growth rate: 1.1%

Currency exchange rate: U.S. $1 = 78.05 Kenyan shillings (2004)

*GDP is the total value of goods and services produced in a country annually.
All figures are 2002 estimates unless otherwise indicated.
Sources: CIA World Factbook, 2003; Bloomberg.com.

than sugar, tea, and coffee flowed out.

By the mid-1980s, the engine of economic growth began to lose steam. A severe drought in 1984 hit the agriculture industry hard and helped create the country's first *trade deficit*. But the end of the steady influx of foreign investment was even more damaging. During this time, the Kenyan government either owned or controlled most of the nation's industries. Foreign companies wishing to launch a business venture in Kenya found that they could not do so without making the government a partner. In addition, corrupt public officials demanded a personal share of the profits. Finding these requirements inconvenient, foreign companies simply stopped investing in Kenya.

Primarily due to international pressure, throughout the 1990s the government sold off its business interests to privately owned companies. Certain industries, such as telecommunications and power generation, still remain government monopolies, but gradually they, too, are being privatized. Despite these measures, foreign investment has not returned to Kenya. Although corruption is on the decline, it remains a deterrent, and foreign companies have also been discouraged by the threat of ethnic violence. (The ethnic bloodshed during the election years of 1992 and 1997 is the most-cited example of instability in Kenya.) More recently, the grim specter of terrorism has been a greater source of anxiety following the 2002 suicide bombing of a hotel in Mombasa.

Islamist terrorists have attacked several targets in Kenya. Suicide bombers hit this Israeli-owned hotel in Mombasa in November 2002. Four years earlier, al-Qaeda terrorists attacked the U.S. Embassy in Nairobi.

The Economy Today

Unstable international markets for coffee and other traditional products have forced Kenya to broaden its scope of exports.

Horticulture, or the production of flowers, fruits, and vegetables, is a prime example of this trend. Between 1995 and 2001, horticulture exports grew by more than 153 percent. The increase in 2002 was nearly 43 percent, and Kenya is now the leading supplier of cut flowers to Europe. Horticulture ranks second behind tea in export revenue for Kenya. These exports and other agricultural goods are vulnerable to the country's frequently harsh weather. Cycles of torrential rainfall and severe drought play havoc with agriculture and other climate-sensitive industries.

Another important but struggling export is coffee. Worldwide supply and demand for coffee fluctuates, occasionally leading to price slumps, but the nation's coffee growers have also been accused of creating their own problems through mismanagement. Regardless, Kenyan coffee is known around the globe for its rich flavor and will always be a major export.

Tourism is a major source of Kenya's revenue, though it has fallen behind in recent years. Escalating crime rates and diminishing wildlife populations are no doubt causes of this decline, but the threat of terrorist attack is the main factor. In 1996, tourism brought $448 million into the country, but by 2002 that figure had dropped to $290 million.

The tourism industry appeared to be making a modest comeback in early 2003, but then in May and June of that year, British Airways temporarily suspended its flights to Kenya after receiving terrorist threats. The industry lost an estimated $13 million a week during that period. Despite the downturn, tourism remains a key industry, inviting over a million visitors to Kenya in 2002.

Kenya has no known natural oil deposits and therefore relies heavily on imported petroleum. In 2002, petroleum products accounted for more than a quarter of the country's total imports. The country also has little in the way of mineral resources. Other major import items include industrial supplies, machinery, and transportation equipment. Kenya's leading trading partner is its former colonial ruler, the United Kingdom.

The United States and Kenya also maintain friendly ties, which in turn bolster significant trade. The U.S. government permits the import of Kenyan products—such as flowers and leather—without tax or tariff as part of the 2000 Africa Growth and Opportunity Act. In 2002, over $188 million in Kenyan goods arrived in America. This figure pales in comparison to the $271 million of American products exported to Kenya during that same year, resulting in a U.S. trade surplus of nearly $83 million. American products that Kenya imports include aircraft and aircraft parts, fertilizers, corn, and wheat. Roughly 100 American companies have offices in Kenya.

Despite their cordial relations, the two nations have to deal with a few contentious issues. Specifically, the United States is worried about Kenya's corruption problem and its vulnerability to terrorism. In recent years, Kenyan officials have been most troubled by a travel advisory that the U.S. State

A young Kenyan girl holds a handful of freshly picked coffee beans. Kenyan coffee is well known for its rich flavor. Although coffee is an important export, the demand for it fluctuates, which can make it a somewhat unreliable source of income.

Department issued after the attacks in 2002. President Kibaki lobbied hard during his first year in office to have the travel advisory lifted, claiming that it was crippling his country's tourism industry.

The United States acknowledged Kenya's ongoing efforts to improve security and pledged additional aid to assist in that goal, but has declined to lift the advisory in the near term. Most security experts agree that Kenya's location and porous borders make it susceptible to terrorist activity. In November 2003, Kenyan police arrested more than 25 suspects in connection with the 1998 car bombing of the U.S. Embassy in Nairobi.

Kenya manages much of its relations with neighboring countries through the East African Community, which Kenya belongs to along with Uganda and Tanzania. This economic alliance allows free trade between member nations. Kenya and its partners have benefited from this arrangement, and other African nations have expressed interest in joining the community.

Roads and Rails

During the 1960s and 1970s, Kenya had the most modern and advanced *infrastructure* in East Africa. Crops raised in the highlands were efficiently transported via road or rail to the developed seaport at Mombasa. New electricity plants powered cities and industrial areas. Airports were constructed to bring in tourists and fly out cargo. The Kenyan economy flourished under the support of a strong infrastructure.

Rather than invest some of its profits in maintenance and improvements, the Moi administration chose to ignore the country's infrastructure, which gradually deteriorated during the 1980s and 1990s. When occasional repairs were authorized, inspectors often took bribes to overlook shoddy work by contractors. The results of this neglect became obvious in 1997, when heavy rains washed away a number of Kenya's weakened roads. By 2000, an alarming 43 percent of the country's road network was deemed virtually unusable. The government responded by launching a $245-million road restoration project, but it was cancelled in 2002 amid accusations of fraud and mismanagement.

Transportation is not the only issue. Aging power plants frequently break down, resulting in outages and brownouts. Water treatment facilities no longer function properly, making fresh drinking water a scarce commodity. Phone service is deficient and overly priced. Improving the national infrastructure remains crucial, particularly for maintaining foreign investment. Between 2001 and 2003, more than 140 foreign companies cited poor infrastructure as a primary reason for pulling out of Kenya.

Labor Shortage

Against this dismal background, the country's 10 million workers must try to find and keep jobs. Kenya's workforce is skilled and well educated, but there are simply not enough jobs for everyone. The unemployment rate has been estimated at 40 percent or higher. People fortunate enough to have a steady job still struggle financially. The average Kenyan worker earns only 23,625 *shillings* a year, or about $300.

The job shortage is due in large part to the country's alarming population growth, which ranks among the highest in the world. Each year, a new wave of recent graduates strikes out in search of employment, only to find little or no work. In past decades, the government absorbed these young workers by

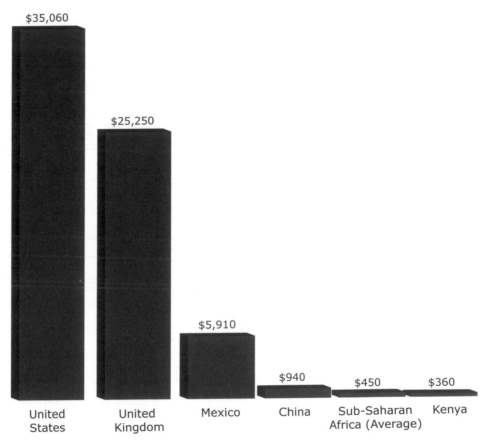

Gross National Income (GNI) Per Capita of Kenya and Other Countries*

United States	$35,060
United Kingdom	$25,250
Mexico	$5,910
China	$940
Sub-Saharan Africa (Average)	$450
Kenya	$360

*Gross national income per capita is the total value of all goods and services produced domestically in a year, supplemented by income received from abroad, divided by midyear population. The above figures take into account fluctuations in currency exchange rates and differences in inflation rates across global economies.

All figures are 2002 estimates. Source: World Bank, 2003.

giving them jobs in public agencies or nationally owned industries. But privatization of the industries has eliminated that option, and few private employers are in need of new hires.

High unemployment and an entrepreneurial spirit have combined to create an informal work sector in Kenya. This industry is known as *jua kali* (literally, "fierce sun"), because at one point many of its workers labored out in the open air under a beating sun. Most *jua kali* businesses now operate indoors and specialize in light manufacturing, which includes the assembly of window frames, charcoal stoves, furniture, and other simple items. These low-budget and often temporary workshops are believed to employ at least 3.7 million people.

To help Kenya overcome its trade deficits, ailing infrastructure, and unemployment, the international community has provided billions of dollars in loans and grants over the years. Although much of this foreign aid was withheld near the end of the Moi administration due to concerns about corruption, donor nations have been pleased thus far with President Kibaki's anti-corruption efforts, and support payments have been resumed.

Kenya is home to many ethnic groups that hold different traditions and customs. (Opposite) Members of the Kikuyu tribe dance on Madaraka Day. The Kikuyu is the largest tribe in Kenya, with approximately 7 million members. (Right) Many of the Luo, the third-largest tribe in Kenya, are fishermen because their homeland is near Lake Victoria.

5 One Nation, Many Cultures

A WIDE ARRAY of peoples settled in the Kenyan region during its early history. That legacy has survived with present-day Kenya's diversity. Most experts agree that no fewer than 34 native ethnic groups reside in the country. Depending on the method of classification that is used, there could be many more groups.

These peoples all share a similar appearance, so language is most often the defining characteristic. Anthropologists have sorted Kenya's numerous languages into three broad categories, according to ancient origin: Bantu-speaking, Nilotic-speaking, and Cushitic-speaking. Bantu-speakers, the largest group, include the Kikuyu, Luhya, and Swahili.

With a population of nearly 7 million, the Kikuyu tribe is the largest and most influential. Roughly one in five Kenyans is Kikuyu. Adaptive

47

Quick Facts: The People of Kenya

Population: 31,639,091

Ethnic groups: Kikuyu 22%, Luhya 14%, Luo 13%, Kalenjin 12%, Kamba 11%, Kisii 6%, Meru 6%, other African 15%, non-African (Asian, European, and Arab) 1%

Age structure:
0–14 years: 41.3%
15–64 years: 55.8%
65 years and over: 2.9%

Population growth rate: 1.27%

Birth rate: 28.81 births/1,000 population

Infant mortality rate: 63.36 deaths/1,000 live births

Death rate: 16.01 deaths/1,000 population

Life expectancy at birth:
total population: 45.22 years
male: 45.43 years
female: 45.83 years

Total fertility rate: 3.47 children born/woman

Religions: Protestant 45%, Roman Catholic 33%, indigenous beliefs 10%, Muslim 10%, other 2%. (Note: a large majority of Kenyans are Christian, but estimates for the percentage of the population that adheres to Islam or indigenous beliefs vary widely.)

Languages: English (official), Kiswahili (official), numerous indigenous languages

Literacy: 85.1%

All figures are 2003 estimates.
Source: Adapted from CIA World Factbook, 2003.

and politically savvy, the Kikuyu played a major role in Kenya's struggle for independence. They reside in Nairobi and in the highlands, where Kikuyu farmers now employ modern agricultural techniques on land their ancestors used before losing it to white settlers. A typical Kikuyu community consists of several close-knit families, led by a council of elders called the *kiama*.

The second-largest tribe is the Luhya, representing about 14 percent of the overall population. The Luhya are also farmers and are located primarily in western Kenya near the Kakamega Forest. Directly to the south lives the nation's third-largest group, the Nilotic-speaking Luo. Because their homeland borders Lake Victoria, the Luo are known as Kenya's fishermen, yet many prefer the urban lifestyle of Nairobi and Mombasa. Traditionally, Luo men have a separate hut known as a *duol* for discussing politics and community issues in which women are not permitted.

Kenyans take great pride in their heritage of their tribe, but intertribal marriage is also common, and a typical Kenyan family may contain members of two or more tribes. In such instances, an individual's tribal identity is based on his or her ancestral bloodlines. The overlap of ethnic groups, plus the influence of colonial rule, has left most Kenyans multilingual, speaking an indigenous language in addition to the official languages of English and Swahili (formally Kiswahili).

During the push for independence, people began to think of themselves and each other as Kenyans, not just members of a particular tribe. Racial conflict and violence decreased significantly during this period. But in the decades since, longstanding tribal rivalries have reemerged, culminating in ethnic violence during the 1992 and 1997 elections. Although Kenya has seen far less racially motivated bloodshed than other African nations, ethnic violence has still haunted the country throughout its history.

Indigenous groups make up 99 percent of the country's population. The remaining 1 percent includes about 100,000 Asians, many of whom are descendants of colonial railway workers from the 1890s. Others can trace their roots to traders and shopkeepers who settled in Kenya centuries ago.

Interestingly, the Asian community remains an important and respected part of Kenya's business sector today. There are also 34,000 Europeans residing in the country—some the children and grandchildren of British settlers—and a small number of Arabic-speaking peoples living on the coast.

Social Institutions

Christianity is the dominant religion in Kenya. Roughly 45 percent of the population is Protestant and 33 percent is Roman Catholic. At one time, a wide variety of religions was practiced in the country, but European missionaries successfully converted the majority of the population. Indigenous faiths are still practiced in remote parts of the country. Islam, which has always had a following on the coast, is gaining popularity in other parts of the country as well. Kenyan Muslims belong to the Sunni sect and tend to be non-fundamentalist, playing down the stricter tenets of Islam in favor of tolerance.

Kenyans place a special emphasis on education. The country's literacy rate of 85 percent is among the highest in Africa, though it lags far behind modernized nations. Widespread poverty has kept many children out of the classroom because their parents simply cannot afford the tuition. Poor rural families often depend on school-age boys to labor in the fields and girls to stay at home and help raise the younger children. These working youths either miss out on an education entirely, or attend school for just a few hours a day before returning to their duties.

In 2003, the newly elected President Kibaki declared that primary education (grades one through eight) would be free to all Kenyans. In the first

Most of the people of Kenya are Christian, but there are areas with high concentrations of Muslims. In this photo Kenyan Christians are leaving Sunday services at a church in Mombasa, an area where 70 percent of the people are Muslims.

week alone, 1.5 million new pupils showed up for class, flooding the country's 17,000 public schools. Already struggling with overcrowded classrooms, Kenya's 175,000 teachers did the best they could to deal with the surge of new students. Classes were held outdoors under shade trees, and some schools began operating in shifts. Kenyans wonder if President Kibaki

Kimani Ng'ang'a Maruge, an 84-year-old former freedom fighter, takes advantage of Kenya's new policy of free primary education, instituted in 2003. He enrolled in the Kapkenduiywo primary school in January 2004 to learn how to read and write.

will be able to maintain his promise of free education. Both the Kenyatta and Moi administrations attempted similar programs in the past, but were forced to reinstate tuition and fees when the costs became too great.

With the possible exception of Nairobi, Kenyan communities lack modern health care. Hospitals are generally understaffed and poorly equipped. Outbreaks of cholera and malaria are common, but the country's most urgent health problem is undoubtedly the HIV/AIDS pandemic. In 2001, an estimated 520 Kenyans died each day from the illness. By 2003 there were roughly 700 AIDS-related deaths per day, and more than one million Kenyan children had been orphaned. The government and international organizations are scrambling to contain the epidemic, but so far have achieved only moderate results.

In the midst of the country's health care crisis, there have been a few notable success stories. One American drug corporation has sponsored a personal hygiene program in 300 Kenyan schools. The program teaches pupils important disease prevention methods, ranging from washing hands after bathroom use to HIV/AIDS avoidance. Students are then asked to pass those lessons on to family members at home. Since the program was instituted in 1998, schools have reported lower absenteeism rates and fewer student illnesses.

Adrecus Miruka, chairman of the community health workers of Masogo, lectures women in his shop about protecting themselves from HIV. In Kenya, as in other countries of East Africa, the spread of AIDS has become a major crisis.

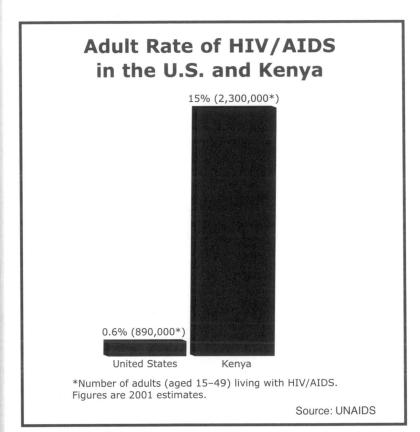

Adult Rate of HIV/AIDS in the U.S. and Kenya

15% (2,300,000*)

0.6% (890,000*)

United States   Kenya

*Number of adults (aged 15–49) living with HIV/AIDS.
Figures are 2001 estimates.

Source: UNAIDS

Culture and Entertainment

Kenyan literature dates back to the 17th century, when Swahili poetry first developed. Most Swahili poems are about love or the virtues of Islam. Perhaps Kenya's most famous modern poet is Shaaban Robert (1909–1962), whose narrative poems are instructive as well as entertaining. The novel is a newer form of literature in Kenya, and Ngugi wa Thiong'o has done much to popularize it. In 1964, Thiong'o published his first novel, *Weep Not, Child*, after which he began writing controversial anti-government literature. Having made many political enemies through his writings, he fled Kenya in 1982. Thiong'o spent several years in England before arriving to the United States to teach at the university level. He has since returned to Kenya and still writes today.

Folk tales also have a special place in the country's history. The stories have been typically told to entertain children at night. Many tales focus on the adventures of animal characters and conclude with a moral lesson. They provide rare insight into local life prior to the 20th century.

Each ethnic group has its own traditional music for celebrating marriages, births, and other important events. A separate kind of music—though just as popular—is gospel, enjoyed by Kenya's many Christians. Nightclub bands play a style of music known as *benga*, which combines ancient tribal melodies with the sounds of modern-day instruments. The Luo were the first people to develop this kind of music in the 1950s. Shirati Jazz is a *benga* band that enjoyed most of its popularity in the 1970s, though it is still one of the best-known groups in the country today.

Kenya has more than 30 magazines and journals, as well as a number of daily newspapers, which operate free of government interference. There is a total of seven television stations, but only the government-owned Kenya Broadcasting Corporation covers the entire nation. Programming consists largely of Western-made reruns, especially American shows. American sitcoms, soap operas, and reality shows are popular among Kenyan viewers, though if there were more available funds, there would likely be more Kenyan-produced programming.

Some Kenyans worry about constant exposure to Western television. They fear that indigenous tradition, fashion, and language will all be diluted by Western influence, and perhaps someday forgotten entirely. This concern has existed since colonial times, when government officials imposed British methods and customs on Kenyan society. Remnants of those century-old conventions still exist today, and until recently, members of the National Assembly were required in house sessions to wear Western-style

In Kenya, independent newspapers, magazines, and journals are generally free from government interference. The front-page story on these Kenyan newspapers refers to a ban on flights to Kenya by British Airways, which was imposed during May–June 2003 for fear of terrorist attacks.

suits instead of their traditional garb.

In recent years there has been a renewed appreciation for traditional Kenyan culture, with traditional clothing gaining popularity in Nairobi, radio stations playing more songs by local bands, and Kenyan-produced films and plays drawing larger audiences. In 2002, native author Binyavanga Wainaina gained recognition for Kenyan literature by receiving the Caine Prize for African Writing. Hoping to build on this renewed sense of national pride, President Kibaki has taken the unprecedented step of asking for input from the arts community before drafting Kenya's cultural policy. These developments have given hope to those concerned about preserving native culture.

Sports

The wide variety of sports in Kenya reflects the country's diverse landscape and its colonial heritage.

European sporting events such as rugby matches, horse racing, and dog shows are popular. Other events such as golf tournaments and deep-sea fishing tournaments exist largely for the tourist trade. Among native Kenyans, soccer (or football, as it is more commonly known outside North America) is easily the most popular sport. The country has two professional soccer leagues, which play to packed stadiums each weekend.

Kenyans have a longstanding international reputation as long-distance runners, traveling around the world to enter and frequently win major marathons. Their reputation first emerged in 1968, when a small contingent of Kenyan runners took home eight Olympic medals. Since then, the country's athletes have collected more than 40 Olympic track medals and set several world records. In recent years, some of Kenya's best athletes have become citizens of other nations to compete as fully paid professionals.

(Opposite) Nairobi is Kenya's capital and largest city, with more than 2.5 million inhabitants. No other city in Kenya is even half its size. (Right) Passengers ride a *matatu*, or minibus taxi. New government rules passed in February 2004 required public transportation vehicles to upgrade safety equipment, reduce speeds, and limit passengers.

6 A Tour of the Cities

ONCE STOPS ALONG ancient trade routes, Mombasa, Malindi, and other coastal cities of Kenya have existed for centuries. Farther inland, most cities are newer, having been founded during the colonial period. The designs of these cities harken back to the European towns the settlers left behind, while the architecture of the coastal cities reflects more of the African and Middle Eastern cultures.

The capital city of Nairobi, in the southern highlands, is easily Kenya's largest metropolis, with a population of more than 2.5 million in 2004. No other city in Kenya is even half that size. A few cities, such as Kisumu in the west, have experienced a declining population as a result of economic downturn. But most are rapidly expanding as the population grows and workers migrate from the countryside in search of employment.

A common sight in all cities is the ***matatu***, Kenya's unique version of a taxi. The name *matatu* comes from the Swahili word for "three," because it typically costs three shillings for a ride. Matatus are a staple of city life in Kenya because most residents cannot afford cars and public transportation is scarce. According to some estimates, there are more than 25,000 matatus on Kenya's roads, meeting a remarkable 70 percent of the country's land transportation needs.

Matatus are convenient, but the reckless habits of their drivers give Kenya the highest road accident fatality rate in the world. Every year more than 3,000 Kenyans perish in motor vehicle accidents. No one is safe from the carnage—not even President Kibaki, who during his 2002 election campaign suffered injuries in a car accident with a matatu. He had to be sworn into office in a wheelchair.

Nairobi

In 1899, when British rail engineers decided to set up a supply depot at Mile 327 in the southern highlands, they probably did not expect it would undergo any expansion. The swampy land was dreary, mosquito-infested, and miles from civilization. Yet the bleak little outpost persisted despite a plague epidemic and a fire. Soon it was a major stop along the railway and a center for trade. Shops and businesses popped up, immigrants from Asia and Europe arrived, and the colonial government set up its offices. The city of Nairobi was born.

Little more than a century later, Nairobi is now the largest metropolis in East Africa. With a continually growing population, estimated at 2,504,400 in 2004, Nairobi is a major hub of African commerce and finance. On its exterior the city appears modern and Western, with glass skyscrapers and fast food restaurants. But unlike most urban areas, it has an abundance of trees and open green spaces. The administrators of the colonial years lined Nairobi's dusty roads with imported trees that still tower overhead today.

Although the city's location was chosen randomly, it proved to be an appropriate spot for the nation's capital. Nairobi borders the traditional tribal land of three different ethnic groups: the Kamba, Kikuyu, and Masai.

In the early years, wild animals frequently wandered off the plains and into town. Unwilling to share their streets with rhinos and giraffes, residents herded the animals to a common area a few miles southwest. The land was left untouched and eventually turned into the country's first national park. Today, Nairobi National Park visitors can watch wild animals roam and hunt as the city's skyline stands in the background. The National Museum, in the northern part of the city, has become a leading institution on the study of human evolution. It also houses one of the world's finest zoological collections.

The capital is burdened with an exorbitant crime rate and high levels of poverty. Displaced rural workers arrive on a daily basis in search of jobs. Many end up in slums to the east of the city. To the west and the north are affluent suburbs, where residents have increasingly felt threatened by crime and have protected themselves with high walls and security guards.

Mombasa

Kenya's second-largest city, Mombasa, had 777,100 people in 2004. In many ways, it is the reverse image of Nairobi. While the capital rests in the cool, dry highlands, Mombasa simmers on the steamy, tropical coast. Nairobi

Fort Jesus, Mombasa, was built by the Portuguese in 1593. Today the structure houses a museum of coastal antiquities.

is a relatively new city; Mombasa is ancient. Even the frantic pace of business in Nairobi contrasts sharply with the laid-back attitude of the coastal town.

Mombasa is actually an island occupying the better portion of a large bay. An ideal trading port, it has been inhabited for at least 2,000 years. The influence of numerous cultures can be observed in the designs of the city's many mosques, churches, and temples. Most city residents speak Swahili and practice Islam, but centuries of migration to the city have fostered an attitude of understanding and religious tolerance. Industrially, Mombasa is first and foremost a seaport, although in recent decades advances in air transport have somewhat lessened the importance of the seaport. Nonetheless, landlocked Uganda continues to depend heavily on Mombasa for transporting imports and exports. The island also contains one of East Africa's largest oil refineries.

Two sets of giant, aluminum elephant tusks are the city's most famous landmarks. Built in 1952 to commemorate a visit by Queen Elizabeth, the huge tusks arc gracefully over Moi Avenue. Portuguese-built Fort Jesus also still stands today, serving as a stark reminder of Mombasa's bloody history. The November 2002 terror attacks underscored this coastal city's vulnerability to outside aggression.

Nakuru and Kisumu

Like Nairobi, Nakuru and Kisumu—respectively, Kenya's third- and fourth-largest cities—owe their existence to the British railway project. The capital of Rift Valley Province, Nakuru is a bustling town, with a population estimated at 256,300 in 2004. Farmers in the region raise pyrethrums, a kind of chrysanthemum used by insecticide manufacturers. Nearby Lake Nakuru occasionally dries up, leaving high winds to coat the city with white dust from the lakebed.

Nestled on an eastern finger of Lake Victoria, Kisumu was once a thriving port community that shipped goods across the lake into central Africa. The city reached its apex in the late 1960s, coinciding with the formation of the East African Community (EAC). This economic alliance between Kenya, Uganda, and Tanzania transformed Kisumu into a major trading hub, bringing great wealth to the city. The EAC abruptly collapsed in 1977 and Kisumu's prosperity suddenly vanished. Throughout the 1980s and early 1990s, the city gradually fell into disrepair as skilled workers moved away and the infrastructure deteriorated.

Kisumu's residents cheered in 1996 when the EAC was reestablished and the docks again became active. United Nations programs have also used the port to distribute humanitarian aid deep into Africa. Regardless, Kisumu has yet to recover from two decades of neglect. Less than half of its residents have running water, and garbage collection is sporadic at best. As a result, outbreaks of cholera and other diseases are common. The city's once-teeming population has dwindled to just a few hundred thousand. Unfinished building projects, including a molasses refinery and a rice mill, commemorate happier times in Kisumu's history and offer a glimmer of hope for the future.

Other Communities

To the southeast of Kisumu is the affluent town of Kericho. Named after British tea planter John Kerich, the town is celebrated as Kenya's tea capital. An ideal climate, highlighted by daily afternoon rain showers, makes Kericho one of the most productive tea regions in the world. Laborers come from the outlying districts to live and work on the mammoth tea plantations, sending their wages to loved ones back home. Endless rolling hills covered with bright green tea leaves are Kericho's trademark.

Along the northern coastline, near the border with Somalia, is a cluster of islands known as the Lamu Archipelago. The islands share Mombasa's tropical conditions and Swahili history, but all similarities end there. Lamu is a quaint, old-fashioned place where the primary modes of transportation are bicycle and donkey. Archaeological sites dot the islands, and venerated Islamic schools draw students and financial support from Saudi Arabia. Recently, Lamu has been forced to deal with uninvited commercial development, as tourists flock to enjoy its pristine beaches and Old World charm. While residents welcome the economic benefits of tourism, they fear their way of life will be jeopardized.

The town of Meru, near Mount Kenya's base, is primarily a logging community. As its sawmills step up their pace to meet escalating demand for prized Meru oak, conservationists worry that the nearby forest will soon disappear. Meru is also the leading producer of **miraa**, a natural stimulant known in other African countries as *khat*. *Miraa* is a type of shrub bark that when chewed makes the user feel alert and exhilarated. Using *miraa* is legal in Kenya, though many frown upon it, and its use among matatu drivers is believed to be responsible for many road accidents.

Countless small towns and villages line the roads between Kenya's major cities. These communities are as unique and diverse as the landscape itself, preserving a national tradition of cultural multiplicity. Such a tradition seems only fitting for the birthplace of humankind.

Kenya faces tremendous challenges in the coming decades: rampant poverty, the HIV/AIDS epidemic, overpopulation. Yet at the same time there is genuine cause for hope. The new government appears determined to make an honest attempt at addressing the nation's troubles. Encouraged by this promising effort, the international community has stepped forward and offered additional financial support. New technology and medical advances in modernized nations may eventually prove effective against Kenya's problems. But perhaps most importantly, individual Kenyans now sense an opportunity to rise above the misery and despair they have endured for so long.

A Calendar of Kenyan Festivals

January

On January 1, **New Year's Day** is celebrated with family and friends. Activities include singing, dancing, and a major feast.

May

Kenya's workers are honored on May 1, **Labor Day**.

June

On June 1, Kenyans celebrate **Madaraka Day**, the anniversary of the country's first steps toward self-government in 1960.

August

The annual **Cultural Music Festival** typically takes place in August at the International Conference Center in Nairobi. Dancers, musicians, and acrobats perform and compete before an audience that includes many government officials. Afterwards, the president invites competition winners to perform at other important functions.

October

October 20 is observed as **Kenyatta Day**, a holiday honoring the birth of the nation's first leader, Jomo Kenyatta. During the day people remember Kenyatta's lengthy imprisonment in the 1950s as well as the sacrifices that other early Kenyan leaders made.

December

December 12 is **Uhuru/Jamhuri (Independence/Republic) Day**, the anniversary of Kenya's official independence from Britain in 1963. Kenya's leaders typically honor the day by giving speeches. On the 26th, Kenyans celebrate **Boxing Day**, a festival that originated in Great Britain. The traditional custom on this day is to give boxes of presents to the less fortunate.

Religious Observances

Kenya's Muslims and Christians observe a number of important holy days related to their religions. Some of these are on particular days each year (for example, **Christmas**, which is observed on December 25, is the Christian celebration of the birth of Jesus). However, many other major celebrations are held according to a lunar calendar, in which the months correspond to the phases of the moon. A lunar month is shorter than a typical month of the Western calendar. Therefore, the festival dates vary from year to year. Other celebrations are observed seasonally.

A very important month of the Muslim lunar calendar is the ninth month, **Ramadan**. This is a time of sacrifice for devout Muslims. Kenyan Muslims celebrate **Eid al-Fitr** to mark the end of Ramadan. **Eid al-Adha** (Feast of

Sacrifice) takes place in the last month of the Muslim calendar during the hajj period, when Muslims make a pilgrimage to Mecca. The holiday honors the prophet Abraham, who was willing to sacrifice his own son to Allah. Each of these holidays is celebrated with a feast. On Eid al-Adha, families traditionally eat a third of the feast and donate the rest to the poor.

The major Christian festivals on the lunar cycle involve the suffering and death of Jesus Christ. **Ash Wednesday** marks the start of a period of self-sacrifice called **Lent**, which lasts for 40 days. The final eight days of Lent are known as Holy Week. A number of important days are observed, including **Palm Sunday**, which commemorates Jesus' arrival in Jerusalem; **Holy Thursday**, which marks the night of the Last Supper; **Good Friday**, the day of Jesus' death on the cross; and **Easter Monday**, which marks his resurrection. (In Western countries, **Easter** is typically celebrated on the day before.)

Recipes

Chapati (Flat Bread)

(Serves 4 to 5)
2 cups flour
1 tsp. salt
Oil (or butter)

Directions:
1. Sift flour and salt into a bowl. Add enough water to make stiff dough.
2. Knead well and roll out on a floured board into a fairly thick circle. Brush with oil.
3. From the center of the circle, make a cut to one edge. Roll up dough into a cone, press both ends in, and make a ball again. Repeat this process two or three more times.
4. Divide dough into four or five balls and roll each out into a thin circle. Heat a frying pan over moderate temperature and dry out each chapati in the pan quickly.
5. Brush the pan with oil and fry each chapati slowly until golden brown on each side.

Maandazi **(Doughnuts)**

(Makes about 24 small doughnuts)
1 cup flour
1 1/4 tsp. baking powder
2 Tbsp. sugar
Pinch of salt
1 egg
1/4 cup water
Oil

Directions:
1. Sift flour and baking powder together. Add sugar and salt.
2. Beat egg well and add water. Stir egg mixture into flour and mix until soft dough is formed. Add more water if necessary.
3. Knead dough in the bowl until it is smooth but not sticky. Dough should leave the sides of the bowl cleanly. Cover with a towel and let rise in a warm place for about 30 minutes.
4. Roll out dough on a floured board until 1/2-inch thick. Cut into squares, strips, or triangles.
5. Fry in oil until golden brown.
6. Drain on absorbent paper.

Maharagwe

(Serves 4 to 6)
1 cup dried red kidney beans
2 medium-size yellow onions, chopped
1–2 Tbsp. oil
2–3 tomatoes, chopped
1 tsp. salt

2 tsp. turmeric
3 chili peppers, ground into a paste, or
1 1/2 tsp. cayenne pepper
2 cups coconut milk

Directions:
1. In a large pot, cover the beans with water and simmer until they are just tender.
2. Sauté onions in oil until golden brown.
3. Add the remaining ingredients to the pot and simmer several minutes until the beans are very tender and the tomatoes are cooked.
4. Serve plain or over rice.

Peanut Soup

(Serves 10)
1 Tbsp. butter
1 cup chopped onion
2 tsp. fresh ginger root
1 cup chopped raw peanuts
2 cups chicken stock
1/2 cup raisins
1 Tbsp. honey
1/2 cup peanut butter
1 1/2 cups milk
Dash each of cinnamon, cloves, salt, and pepper

Directions:
1. Sauté onion, ginger, salt, and pepper in butter until onions become clear. Add cinnamon, cloves, and peanuts and sauté for 5 to 10 minutes.
2. Stir in chicken stock, raisins, honey, and peanut butter. Mix thoroughly.
3. Cover and simmer over low heat for one hour. Add milk and serve when soup is hot.

Ugali (Cornmeal Porridge)

(Serves 4 to 6)
1 cup cold water
1 cup yellow cornmeal
1 tsp. salt, more or less to taste
3 cups boiling water

Directions:
1. Put cold water in saucepan and add cornmeal and salt, mixing continually.
2. Bring to a boil over high heat and, stirring continuously, slowly add 3 cups boiling water to prevent lumps.
3. Reduce to simmer, cover, and cook for about eight minutes, mixing frequently to prevent sticking. Add salt to taste and mix well.
4. Serve in individual bowls with cream, sugar, syrup, ghee, or butter.

Glossary

benga—originating with the Luo people, a popular style of music that is based on ancient tribal melodies.

duol—a hut where male members of a Luo community meet to discuss issues.

graft—the crime of abusing public office for personal gain.

harambee—means "pulling together" and in Kenya is a common method of raising money for community projects.

horticulture—the production of flowers, fruits, and vegetables.

indigenous—originating and living in a particular region or country.

infrastructure—apparatus vital to economic activity, such as roads and communication networks.

jua kali—literally "fierce sun," this is Kenya's informal manufacturing industry where work is sometimes performed outdoors under the beating sun.

kiama—a Kikuyu council of elders.

Kikuyu—the most populous tribe in Kenya.

kitu-kidogo—Swahili for "a little something," it is the term commonly used to describe a bribe.

matatu—a decorated van used as a taxi, commonly seen in Kenya.

miraa—a legal natural stimulant similar to khat; though *miraa* is legal, many Kenyans disdain the use of it.

nationalist—supporting the goal of a people with a specific identity and culture to achieve independence.

Glossary

poaching—illegal hunting, usually for profit, that can drive a species to extinction if left unchecked.

rainbow coalition—a political organization comprised of diverse groups that seek unity in national government.

savanna—hot, dry grassland that is home to grazing animals and predators.

shilling—Kenya's currency; roughly 79 shillings equal one American dollar.

trade deficit—a negative balance in trade in which a nation's imports exceed its exports.

uhuru—"freedom" in Swahili; this word became a rallying cry during Kenya's quest for independence.

wildebeest—a large antelope that annually migrates across southern Kenya in great numbers; also called a gnu.

Project and Report Ideas

Map

Draw and color a map of Kenya that includes the following landmarks: Mount Kenya, Lake Victoria, Lake Turkana (formerly Lake Rudolf), the Great Rift Valley, Nairobi, and Mombasa. Identify Kenya's borders with Somalia, Ethiopia, Sudan, Uganda, Tanzania, and the Indian Ocean.

Report Ideas

Using an encyclopedia or other reference book, research the life of Kenya's first president, Jomo Kenyatta. Write a two-page biography about Kenyatta. Include information about his youth, his imprisonment by the colonial authorities, and his efforts to make Kenya an independent nation.

Imagine you are a government official who has been placed in charge of Kenya's anti-corruption program. Write a two-page report describing the steps you would take to ensure that government leaders do not abuse their power. How might Kenyan citizens take part in the fight against corruption? Could Kenyan newspapers and television help?

Write a two-page report about the British colonization of Kenya. Your report should answer the following questions: In what ways was colonization harmful to Kenya? What were some positive effects of colonization? How do you think Kenya might be different today had it not been colonized?

Project and Report Ideas

Creative Project

Using newspapers, magazines, and the Internet, find pictures of Kenya's wildlife, landscape, and people. Make a poster with these images and write a caption for each picture. Create a title for your poster, and decorate it with drawings of the Kenyan national flag and anything else you would like to include.

Presentation

Plan an imaginary trip for yourself to Kenya. Prepare an oral presentation for your class about the trip. Name the three places you would like to visit most and point them out on a map of Kenya, explaining why they interest you. Show an interesting picture that is related to each location.

Chronology

500 B.C.–A.D. 500	Bantu-speaking peoples migrate to Kenya from Sudan and western Africa.
ca. 700	Arabs settle along the Kenyan coast and establish trading centers with the rest of the Arab world.
ca. 750	Swahili settlements are set up along the Kenyan coast.
1498	Portuguese explorer Vasco da Gama arrives.
1500–1600	The Portuguese establish rule in the Kenyan coastal region.
1696–99	Mombasa residents lay siege to Fort Jesus, killing hundreds of Portuguese defenders.
1885	Britain claims authority over Kenya.
1887	The British East Africa Company is founded.
1896–1902	The British build a railway from Mombasa to Lake Victoria.
1944	The Kenyan African Union (KAU) is formed, with the objective of working toward Kenyan independence.
1952	The Mau Mau Rebellion is launched and the government declares a state of emergency; Jomo Kenyatta and other leaders are imprisoned.
1961	The British make preparations to grant the colony independence; Jomo Kenyatta is released from prison; a provisional Kenyan government is formed.
1963	Kenya officially gains independence.
1964	Kenya becomes a republic with Kenyatta as president.
1978	Kenyatta dies and is succeeded by Daniel arap Moi.

1982   A coup attempt by junior officers of the Kenyan Air Force fails.

1989   Richard Leakey is named head of Kenya Wildlife Service; the crackdown on poaching begins.

1991   The government introduces a multiparty political system.

1992   Daniel arap Moi is re-elected in multiparty elections.

1997   Moi is reelected to another five-year term amid significant fraud and violence.

1998   A car bomb destroys U.S. Embassy in Nairobi; over 200 are killed and thousands wounded.

2002   Terror attacks near Mombasa in November kill 13 people; in December, Mwai Kibaki is elected president, ending Moi's 24-year rule, and vows to end government corruption.

2003   The HIV/AIDS epidemic is declared a national disaster, with 14 percent of the population infected; the government bans public officials from managing *harambees*; in October, a government probe leads to the suspension of 23 judges for unethical conduct.

2004   In February, many legislators declare that they will continue to manage *harambees* despite the 2003 law.

2005   In March, Amnesty International issues a report accusing the Kenyan government of human-rights violations in its treatment of people arrested on suspicion of terrorist activities.

Further Reading/Internet Resources

Bindloss, Joseph, et al. *Lonely Planet: Kenya*. Melbourne, Aus.: Lonely Planet Publications, 2003.

Gilbert, Elizabeth L. *Broken Spears: A Maasai Journey*. New York: Atlantic Monthly Press, 2003.

Kilbride, Philip, Collette Suda, and Enos Njeru. *Street Children in Kenya: Voices of Children in Search of a Childhood*. Westport, Conn.: Bergin & Garvey, 2000.

Leakey, Richard, and Virginia Morell. *Wildlife Wars: My Fight to Save Africa's Natural Treasures*. New York: St. Martin's Press, 2001.

Pike, Jeffrey. *Insight Guide: Kenya*. Maspeth, N.Y.: APA Publications, 1999.

Trillo, Richard. *The Rough Guide to Kenya*. London: Rough Guides, 2002.

Travel Information

http://www.magicalkenya.com
http://www.kenyalogy.com

History and Geography

http://www.mfa.go.ke/index.html
http://www.kws.org
http://www.africaguide.com/country/kenya/index.htm

Economic and Political Information

http://www.kenyaembassy.com
http://www.statehousekenya.go.ke
http://www.treasury.go.ke

Culture and Festivals

http://www.kenyaweb.com
http://www.kenya-travel-safari.com/kenya-festivals

Embassy of the Republic of Kenya
2249 R Street, NW
Washington, DC 20008
(202) 387-6101

Kenya Tourist Board
Carlson Destination Marketing Services
P.O. Box 59159
Minneapolis, MN 55459-8257
1-866-44-KENYA

The National Assembly
Parliament Buildings, Parliament Road
P.O. Box 41842
Nairobi
Republic of Kenya
(254) 221291

Kenya Wildlife Service
P.O. Box 40241
Nairobi
Republic of Kenya
(254) 020-600800

Index

Africa Growth and Opportunity
    Act, 41
agriculture, *37*, 38, 40
    See also economy
AIDS/HIV, 52–53, *54*
arap Moi, Daniel. *See* Moi,
    Daniel arap

British East Africa Company, 21
    See also Great Britain
Bunge. *See* National Assembly
    (Bunge)

climate, 13–14
coffee, 39, 40, *41*
    See also economy
colonialism (European), 19–23,
    24–25
corruption, 25, 33–34, 38–39,
    41–42
crocodiles (Nile), 16–17
    See also wildlife
culture, 50–57

da Gama, Vasco. *See* Gama,
    Vasco da

East African Community (EAC),
    42, 63–64
economy, 37–45
education, 50–52
    See also culture

elections, 26–27, 29, 32
    See also government
elephant (African), 14, 17
    See also wildlife
ethnic groups, 21, 22, 23–24, 25,
    47–50, 55

foreign aid, 26
Fort Jesus, Mombasa, 20, *62*, 63

Gama, Vasco da, 20, *21*
geographic features, 11–13
Germany, 21
government, 25, 27, 29–33
Great Britain, 20–23, 24, 26
Great Rift Valley, 12
gross national income (GNI), 44
    See also economy

harambee, 30–31
health care, 52–53, *54*
hippopotamus, 15
    See also wildlife
history
    colonialism (European),
        20–22
    under Daniel arap Moi,
        25–27
    independence, 22–25
    Mau Mau Rebellion, 23–24
    prehistoric humans, 19–20
HIV/AIDS, 52–53, 54
horticulture. *See* agriculture

independence, 23–25
    See also history
infrastructure, 42–43

judicial system, 30
    See also government

Kakamega Forest, 49
Kenya
    cities, 59–65
    climate, 13–14
    culture, 50–57
    economy, 37–45
    geographic features, 11–13
    government, 25, 27, 29–33
    history, 19–27
    independence, 23–25
    infrastructure, 42–43
    population, 43, 47, 48, 49, 59,
        60, 61, 63
    wildlife, 14–17, 34–35
Kenya African National Union
    (KANU), 31, *32*
    See also political parties
Kenya Wildlife Service (KWS),
    34–35
    See also wildlife
Kenyan African Union (KAU),
    23, 31
    See also political parties
Kenyatta, Jomo, 23, 24–25, *26*, *27*,
    31
Kerich, John, 64

Numbers in **bold italic** refer to captions.

Kericho, 64
Kibaki, Mwai, 27, *29*, 31–32, 33, 42, 45, 50–51, 56, 60
Kikuyu, 22, 23–24, 25, 47–48
    See also ethnic groups
Kikuyu Central Association (KCA), 31
    See also political parties
Kisumu, 59, 63–64
kitu-kidogo, 33–34
    See also corruption

bin Laden, Osama, 27
Lake Rudolf. *See* Lake Turkana
Lake Turkana, 12
Lake Victoria, 12
Lamu Archipelago, 64–65
languages, 11, 19–20, 47, 49
Leakey, Richard, 34–35
literature, 54–55, 56
    See also culture
Luhya, 48–49
    See also ethnic groups
Luo, *47*, 49, 55
    See also ethnic groups

Masai, *19*, 21
    See also ethnic groups
Malindi, 59
Maruge, Kimani Ng'ang'a, *52*
Mau Mau Rebellion, 23–24, *26*, 31
    See also history

media, 55–56
    See also culture
Meru, 65
Miruka, Adrecus, *53*
Moi, Daniel arap, 25–26, *27*, *29*, 31–32
Mombasa, 20, 21, 42, 59, 61–62
    terrorist attacks in, 27, 39, 63
Mount Kenya, *11*, 12, 65
music, 55
    See also culture

Nairobi, 21, *29*, 59, 60–61
    terrorist attack in, 27, *39*, 42
Nairobi National Park, 61
Nakaru, 63
National Assembly (Bunge), 29–30
    See also government
National Rainbow Coalition (NARC), 32
    See also political parties
nationalism. *See* independence

political parties, 27, 31–32
    See also government
population, 43, 47, 48, 49, 59, 60, 61, 63
Portugal, 20, *21*
prehistoric humans, 11, 19, 34

al-Qaeda, 27, *39*

religion, 50, *51*
    See also culture
rhinoceros (African black), 14, *15*, 17
    See also wildlife
Robert, Shaaban, 54

sports, 56–57
    See also culture
Sweetwaters Game Reserve, *15*
    See also wildlife

terrorism, 26–27, 39, 40, 42
Thiong'o, Ngugi wa, 54
tourism, *16*, 35, 40
    See also economy
Transparency International, 33
tribes. *See* ethnic groups

Uhuru (Freedom) Movement, 25
unemployment rate, 43, 45
    See also economy
United States, 26, 41–42

Wainaina, Binyavanga, 56
wildebeest, 14–15
    See also wildlife
wildlife, 14–17, 34–35
World War I, 22
World War II, 23

Contributors/Picture Credits

Professor Robert I. Rotberg is Director of the Program on Intrastate Conflict and Conflict Resolution at the Kennedy School, Harvard University, and President of the World Peace Foundation. He is the author of a number of books and articles on Africa, including *A Political History of Tropical Africa* and *Ending Autocracy, Enabling Democracy: The Tribulations of Southern Africa.*

Jim Corrigan has authored numerous newspaper and magazine articles, as well as several nonfiction books for students. A full-time freelance writer, Corrigan specializes in topics relating to history, travel, and ethnic studies. His books for young readers include *The Civil War in the West, Europeans and Native Americans,* and *Filipino Immigration.* He is a graduate of Penn State University and currently resides near Harrisburg, Pennsylvania.